# WALT WHITMAN

Selected
Poems

BLOOMSBURY
★ POETRY ★
CLASSICS

St. Martin's Press
New York

*Jacket design by Jeff Fisher*

Library of Congress Cataloging-in-Publication Data
Whitman, Walt, 1819–1892.
[Poems. Selections]
Selected poems / Walt Whitman.
p.    cm. — (Bloomsbury poetry classics)
ISBN 0-312-09754-9
I. Title.    II. Series.
PS3204    1993b
811'.3—dc20        93-25505        CIP

Selection by Ian Hamilton
First published in Great Britain by Bloomsbury Publishing Ltd.

10 9 8 7 6 5 4 3

# CONTENTS

## SHUT NOT YOUR DOORS

Shut not your doors to me proud libraries,
For that which was lacking on all your well-fill'd
   shelves, yet needed most, I bring,
Forth from the war emerging, a book I have made,
The words of my book nothing, the drift of it every
   thing,
A book separate, not link'd with the rest nor felt by
   the intellect,
But you ye untold latencies will thrill to every page.

# BEGINNERS

How they are provided for upon the earth, (appearing
    at intervals,)
How dear and dreadful they are to the earth,
How they inure to themselves as much as to any –
    what a paradox appears their age,
How people respond to them, yet know them not,
How there is something relentless in their fate all
    times,
How all times mischoose the objects of their adulation
    and reward,
And how the same inexorable price must still be paid
    for the same great purchase.

## ON JOURNEYS THROUGH THE STATES

On journeys through the States we start,
(Ay through the world, urged by these songs,
Sailing henceforth to every land, to every sea,)
We willing learners of all, teachers of all, and lovers of
    all.

We have watch'd the seasons dispensing themselves
    and passing on,
And have said, Why should not a man or woman do
    as much as the seasons, and effuse as much?

We dwell a while in every city and town,
We pass through Kanada, the North-east, the vast
    valley of the Mississippi, and the Southern States,
We confer on equal terms with each of the States,
We make trial of ourselves and invite men and women
    to hear,
We say to ourselves, Remember, fear not, be candid,
    promulge the body and the soul,
Dwell a while and pass on, be copious, temperate,
    chaste, magnetic,
And what you effuse may then return as the seasons
    return,
And may be just as much as the seasons.

## TO YOU

Stranger, if you passing meet me and desire to speak
   to me, why should you not speak to me?
And why should I not speak to you?

*From* STARTING FROM PAUMANOCK

4.

Take my leaves America, take them South and take
 them North,
Make welcome for them everywhere, for they are your
 own offspring,
Surround them East and West, for they would
 surround you,
And you precedents, connect lovingly with them, for
 they connect lovingly with you.

I conn'd old times,
I sat studying at the feet of the great masters,
Now if eligible O that the great masters might return
 and study me.

In the name of these States shall I scorn the antique?
Why these are the children of the antique to justify it.

## 9.

What do you seek so pensive and silent?
What do you need camerado?
Dear son do you think it is love?

Listen dear son – listen America, daughter or son,
It is a painful thing to love a man or woman to excess,
   and yet it satisfies, it is great,
But there is something else very great, it makes the
   whole coincide,
It, magnificent, beyond materials, with continuous
   hands sweeps and provides for all.

## 12.

Democracy! near at hand to you a throat is now
  inflating itself and joyfully singing.

Ma femme! for the brood beyond us and of us,
For those who belong here and those to come,
I exultant to be ready for them will now shake out
  carols stronger and haughtier than have ever yet
  been heard upon earth.

I will make the songs of passion to give them their
  way,
And your songs outlaw'd offenders, for I scan you with
  kindred eyes, and carry you with me the same as
  any.

I will make the true poem of riches,
To earn for the body and the mind whatever adheres
  and goes forward and is not dropt by death;
I will effuse egotism and show it underlying all, and I
  will be the bard of personality,
And I will show of male and female that either is but
  the equal of the other.

And sexual organs and acts! do you concentrate in
    me, for I am determin'd to tell you with courageous
    clear voice to prove you illustrious,
And I will show that there is no imperfection in the
    present, and can be none in the future,
And I will show that whatever happens to anybody it
    may be turn'd to beautiful results,
And I will show that nothing can happen more
    beautiful than death,
And I will thread a thread through my poems that
    time and events are compact,
And that all the things of the universe are perfect
    miracles, each as profound as any.

I will not make poems with reference to parts,
But I will make poems, songs, thoughts, with reference
    to ensemble,
And I will not sing with reference to a day, but with
    reference to all days,

And I will not make a poem nor the least part of a
poem but has reference to the soul,
Because having look'd at the objects of the universe, I
find there is no one nor any particle of one but has
reference to the soul.

*From* SONG OF MYSELF

1.

I celebrate myself, and sing myself,
And what I assume you shall assume,
For every atom belonging to me as good belongs to
   you.

I loafe and invite my soul,
I lean and loafe at my ease observing a spear of
   summer grass.

My tongue, every atom of my blood, form'd from this
   soil, this air,
Born here of parents born here from parents the same,
   and their parents the same,
I, now thirty-seven years old in perfect health begin,
Hoping to cease not till death.

Creeds and schools in abeyance,
Retiring back a while sufficed at what they are, but
   never forgotten,
I harbor for good or bad, I permit to speak at every
   hazard,
Nature without check with original energy.

## 5.

I believe in you my soul, the other I am must not
    abase itself to you,
And you must not be abased to the other.

Loafe with me on the grass, loose the stop from your
    throat,
Not words, not music or rhyme I want, not custom or
    lecture, not even the best,
Only the lull I like, the hum of your valvèd voice.

I mind how once we lay such a transparent summer
    morning,
How you settled your head athwart my hips and
    gently turn'd over upon me,
And parted the shirt from my bosom-bone, and
    plunged your tongue to my bare-stript heart,
And reach'd till you felt my beard, and reach'd till you
    held my feet.

Swiftly arose and spread around me the peace and
    knowledge that pass all the argument of the earth,
And I know that the hand of God is the promise of
    my own,

And I know that the spirit of God is the brother of
   my own,
And that all the men ever born are also my brothers,
   and the women my sisters and lovers,
And that a kelson of the creation is love,
And limitless are leaves stiff or drooping in the fields,
And brown ants in the little wells beneath them,
And mossy scabs of the worm fence, heap'd stones,
   elder, mullein and poke-weed.

## 8

The little one sleeps in its cradle,
I lift the gauze and look a long time, and silently brush
  away flies with my hand.

The youngster and the red-faced girl turn aside up the
  bushy hill,
I peeringly view them from the top.

The suicide sprawls on the bloody floor of the
  bedroom,
I witness the corpse with its dabbled hair, I note where
  the pistol has fallen.

The blab of the pave, tires of carts, sluff of boot-soles,
  talk of the promenaders,
The heavy omnibus, the driver with his interrogating
  thumb, the clank of the shod horses on the granite
  floor,
The snow-sleighs, clinking, shouted jokes, pelts of
  snow-balls,
The hurrahs for popular favorites, the fury of rous'd
  mobs,
The flap of the curtain'd litter, a sick man inside borne
  to the hospital,

The meeting of enemies, the sudden oath, the blows
    and fall,
The excited crowd, the policeman with his star quickly
    working his passage to the centre of the crowd,
The impassive stones that receive and return so many
    echoes,
What groans of over-fed or half-starv'd who fall
    sunstruck or in fits,
What exclamations of women taken suddenly who
    hurry home and give birth to babes,
What living and buried speech is always vibrating
    here, what howls restrain'd by decorum,
Arrests of criminals, slights, adulterous offers made,
    acceptances, rejections with convex lips,
I mind them or the show or resonance of them – I
    come and I depart.

9.

The big doors of the country barn stand open and
    ready,
The dried grass of the harvest-time loads the slow-
    drawn wagon,
The clear light plays on the brown gray and green
    intertinged,
The armfuls are pack'd to the sagging mow.

I am there, I help, I came stretch'd atop of the load,
I felt its soft jolts, one leg reclined on the other,
I jump from the cross-beams and seize the clover and
    timothy,
And roll head over heels and tangle my hair full of
    wisps.

Twenty-eight young men bathe by the shore,
Twenty-eight young men and all so friendly;
Twenty-eight years of womanly life and all so
lonesome.

She owns the fine house by the rise of the bank,
She hides handsome and richly drest aft the blinds of
the window.

Which of the young men does she like the best?
Ah the homeliest of them is beautiful to her.

Where are you off to, lady? for I see you,
You splash in the water there, yet stay stock still in
your room.

Dancing and laughing along the beach came the
twenty-ninth bather,
The rest did not see her, but she saw them and loved
them.

The beards of the young men glisten'd with wet, it ran
    from their long hair,
Little streams pass'd all over their bodies.

An unseen hand also pass'd over their bodies,
It descended tremblingly from their temples and ribs.

The young men float on their backs, their white bellies
    bulge to the sun, they do not ask who seizes fast to
    them,
They do not know who puffs and declines with
    pendant and bending arch,
They do not think whom they souse with spray.

## 14.

The wild gander leads his flock through the cool night,
*Ya-honk* he says, and sounds it down to me like an
    invitation,
The pert may suppose it meaningless, but I listening
    close,
Find its purpose and place up there toward the wintry
    sky.

The sharp-hoof'd moose of the north, the cat on the
    house-sill, the chickadee, the prairie-dog,
The litter of the grunting sow as they tug at her teats,
The brood of the turkey-hen and she with her half-
    spread wings,
I see in them and myself the same old law.

The press of my foot to the earth springs a hundred
    affections,
They scorn the best I can do to relate them.

I am enamour'd of growing out-doors,
Of men that live among cattle or taste of the ocean or
     woods,
Of the builders and steerers of ships and the wielders
     of axes and mauls, and the drivers of horses,
I can eat and sleep with them week in and week out.

What is commonest, cheapest, nearest, easiest, is Me,
Me going in for my chances, spending for vast returns,
Adorning myself to bestow myself on the first that will
     take me,
Not asking the sky to come down to my good will,
Scattering it freely forever.

These are really the thoughts of all men in all ages and
    lands, they are not original with me,
If they are not yours as much as mine they are
    nothing, or next to nothing,
If they are not the riddle and the untying of the riddle
    they are nothing,
If they are not just as close as they are distant they are
    nothing.

This is the grass that grows wherever the land is and
    the water is,
This the common air that bathes the globe.

## 21.

I am the poet of the Body and I am the poet of the
    Soul,
The pleasures of heaven are with me and the pains of
    hell are with me,
The first I graft and increase upon myself, the latter I
    translate into a new tongue.

I am the poet of the woman the same as the man,
And I say it is as great to be a woman as to be a man,
And I say there is nothing greater than the mother of
    men.

I chant the chant of dilation or pride,
We have had ducking and deprecating about enough,
I show that size is only development.

Have you outstript the rest? are you the President?
It is a trifle, they will more than arrive there every
    one, and still pass on.

I am he that walks with the tender and growing night,
I call to the earth and sea half-held by the night.

Press close bare-bosom'd night – press close magnetic
   nourishing night!
Night of south winds – night of the large few stars!
Still nodding night – mad naked summer night.

Smile O voluptuous cool-breath'd earth!
Earth of the slumbering and liquid trees!
Earth of departed sunset – earth of the mountains
   misty-topt!
Earth of the vitreous pour of the full moon just tinged
   with blue!
Earth of shine and dark mottling the tide of the river!
Earth of the limpid gray of clouds brighter and clearer
   for my sake!
Far-swooping elbow'd earth – rich apple-blossom'd
   earth!
Smile, for your lover comes.

Prodigal, you have given me love – therefore I to you
   give love!
O unspeakable passionate love.

Now I will do nothing but listen,
To accrue what I hear into this song, to let sounds
   contribute toward it.


I hear bravuras of birds, bustle of growing wheat,
   gossip of flames, clack of sticks cooking my meals,
I hear the sound I love, the sound of the human voice,
I hear all sounds running together, combined, fused or
   following,
Sounds of the city and sounds out of the city, sounds
   of the day and night,
Talkative young ones to those that like them, the loud
   laugh of work-people at their meals,
The angry base of disjointed friendship, the faint tones
   of the sick,
The judge with hands tight to the desk, his pallid lips
   pronouncing a death-sentence,
The heave'e'yo of stevedores unloading ships by the
   wharves, the refrain of the anchor-lifters,
The ring of alarm-bells, the cry of fire, the whirr of
   swift-streaking engines and hose-carts with
   premonitory tinkles and color'd lights,
The steam-whistle, the solid roll of the train of
   approaching cars,

The slow march play'd at the head of the association
  marching two and two,
(They go to guard some corpse, the flag-tops are
  draped with black muslin.)

I hear the violoncello, ('tis the young man's heart's
  complaint,)
I hear the key'd cornet, it glides quickly in through my
  ears,
It shakes mad-sweet pangs through my belly and
  breast.

I hear the chorus, it is a grand opera,
Ah this indeed is music – this suits me.

A tenor large and fresh as the creation fills me,
The orbic flex of his mouth is pouring and filling me
  full.

I hear the train'd soprano (what work with hers is
    this?)
The orchestra whirls me wider than Uranus flies,
It wrenches such ardors from me I did not know I
    possess'd them,
It sails me, I dab with bare feet, they are lick'd by the
    indolent waves,
I am cut by bitter and angry hail, I lose my breath,
Steep'd amid honey'd morphine, my windpipe
    throttled in fakes of death,
At length let up again to feel the puzzle of puzzles,
And that we call Being.

. . .

I understand the large hearts of heroes,
    The courage of present times and all times,
How the skipper saw the crowded and rudderless
    wreck of the steam-ship, and Death chasing it up
    and down the storm,
How he knuckled tight and gave not back an inch,
    and was faithful of days and faithful of nights,
And chalk'd in large letters on a board, *Be of good
    cheer, we will not desert you;*
How he follow'd with them and tack'd with them
    three days and would not give it up,
How he saved the drifting company at last,
How the lank loose-gown'd women look'd when
    boated from the side of their prepared graves,
How the silent old-faced infants and the lifted sick,
    and the sharp-lipp'd unshaved men;
All this I swallow, it tastes good, I like it well, it
    becomes mine,
I am the man, I suffer'd, I was there.

42.

A call in the midst of the crowd,
My own voice, orotund sweeping and final.

Come my children,
Come my boys and girls, my women, household and
   intimates,
Now the performer launches his nerve, he has pass'd
   his prelude on the reeds within.

Easily written loose-finger'd chords – I feel the thrum
   of your climax and close.

My head slues round on my neck,
Music rolls but not from the organ,
Folks are around me, but they are no household of
   mine.

Ever the hard unsunk ground,
Ever the eaters and drinkers, ever the upward and
    downward sun, ever the air and the ceaseless tides,
Ever myself and my neighbors, refreshing, wicked, real,
Ever the old inexplicable query, ever that thorn'd
    thumb, that breath of itches and thirsts,
Ever the vexer's *hoot! hoot!* till we find where the sly
    one hides and bring him forth,
Ever love, ever the sobbing liquid of life,
Ever the bandage under the chin, ever the trestles of
    death.

Here and there with dimes on the eyes walking,
To feed the greed of the belly the brains liberally
    spooning,
Tickets buying, taking, selling, but in to the feast
    never once going,
Many sweating, ploughing, thrashing, and then the
    chaff for payment receiving,
A few idly owning, and they the wheat continually
    claiming.

This is the city and I am one of the citizens,
Whatever interests the rest interests me, politics, wars,
    markets, newspapers, schools,
The mayor and councils, banks, tariffs, steamships,
    factories, stocks, stores, real estate and personal
    estate.

The little plentiful manikins skipping around in collars
    and tail'd coats,
I am aware who they are, (they are positively not
    worms or fleas,)
I acknowledge the duplicates of myself, the weakest
    and shallowest is deathless with me,
What I do and say the same waits for them,
Every thought that flounders in me the same flounders
    in them.

I know perfectly well my own egotism,

Know my omnivorous lines and must not write any less,

And would fetch you whoever you are flush with myself.


Not words of routine this song of mine,

But abruptly to question, to leap beyond yet nearer bring;

This printed and bound book – but the printer and the printing-office boy?

The well-taken photographs – but your wife or friend close and solid in your arms?

The black ship mail'd with iron, her mighty guns in her turrets – but the pluck of the captain and engineers?

In the houses the dishes and fare and furniture – but the host and hostess, and the look out of their eyes?

The sky up there – yet here or next door, or across the way?

The saints and sages in history – but you yourself?

Sermons, creeds, theology – but the fathomless human brain,

And what is reason? and what is love? and what is life?

## 52.

The spotted hawk swoops by and accuses me, he
   complains of my gab and my loitering.

I too am not a bit tamed, I too am untranslatable,
I sound my barbaric yawp over the roofs of the world.

The last scud of day holds back for me,
It flings my likeness after the rest and true as any on
   the shadow'd wilds,
It coaxes me to the vapor and the dusk.

I depart as air, I shake my white locks at the runaway
   sun,
I effuse my flesh in eddies, and drift it in lacy jags.

I bequeath myself to the dirt to grow from the grass I
   love,
If you want me again look for me under your boot-
   soles.

You will hardly know who I am or what I mean,
But I shall be good health to you nevertheless,
And filter and fibre your blood.

Failing to fetch me at first keep encouraged,
Missing me one place search another,
I stop somewhere waiting for you.

## *From* I SING THE BODY ELECTRIC

### 4.

I have perceiv'd that to be with those I like is enough,
To stop in company with the rest at evening is
    enough,
To be surrounded by beautiful, curious, breathing,
    laughing flesh is enough,
To pass among them or touch any one, or rest my
    arm ever so lightly round his or her neck for a
    moment, what is this then?
I do not ask any more delight, I swim in it as in a sea.

There is something in staying close to men and
    women and looking on them, and in the contact
    and odor of them, that pleases the soul well,
All things please the soul, but these please the soul
    well.

## OUT OF THE ROLLING OCEAN THE CROWD

Out of the rolling ocean the crowd came a drop gently
    to me,
Whispering *I love you, before long I die,*
*I have travel'd a long way merely to look on you to touch*
    *you,*
*For I could not die till I once look'd on you,*
*For I fear'd I might afterward lose you.*

Now we have met, we have look'd, we are safe,
Return in peace to the ocean my love,
I too am part of that ocean my love, we are not so
    much separated,
Behold the great rondure, the cohesion of all, how
    perfect!
But as for me, for you, the irresistible sea is to separate
    us,
As for an hour carrying us diverse, yet cannot carry us
    diverse forever;
Be not impatient – a little space – know you I salute
    the air, the ocean and the land,
Every day at sundown for your dear sake my love.

# WE TWO, HOW LONG WE WERE FOOL'D

We two, how long we were fool'd,
Now transmuted, we swiftly escape as Nature escapes,
We are Nature, long have we been absent, but now we
    return,
We become plants, trunks, foliage, roots, bark,
We are bedded in the ground, we are rocks,
We are oaks, we grow in the openings side by side,
We browse, we are two among the wild herds
    spontaneous as any,
We are two fishes swimming in the sea together,
We are what locust blossoms are, we drop scent
    around lanes mornings and evenings,
We are also the coarse smut of beasts, vegetables,
    minerals,
We are two predatory hawks, we soar above and look
    down,
We are two resplendent suns, we it is who balance
    ourselves orbic and stellar, we are as two comets,
We prowl fang'd and four-footed in the woods, we
    spring on prey,
We are two clouds forenoons and afternoons driving
    overhead,

We are seas mingling, we are two of those cheerful
   waves rolling over each other and interwetting each
   other,
We are what the atmosphere is, transparent, receptive,
   previous, impervious,
We are snow, rain, cold, darkness, we are each
   product and influence of the globe,
We have circled and circled till we have arrived home
   again, we two,
We have voided all but freedom and all but our own
   joy.

## HOURS CONTINUING LONG

Hours continuing long, sore and heavy-hearted,
Hours of the dusk, when I withdraw to a lonesome
  and unfrequented spot, seating myself, leaning my
  face in my hands;
Hours sleepless, deep in the night, when I go forth,
  speeding swiftly the country roads, or through the
  city streets, or pacing miles and miles, stifling
  plaintive cries;
Hours discouraged distracted – for the one I cannot
  content myself without, soon I saw him content
  himself without me;
Hours when I am forgotten, (O weeks and months are
  passing, but I believe I am never to forget!)
Sullen and suffering hours! (I am ashamed – but it is
  useless – I am what I am;)
Hours of my torment – I wonder if other men ever
  have the like, out of the like feelings?
Is there even one other like me – distracted – his
  friend, his lover, lost to him?
Is he too as I am now? Does he still rise in the
  morning, dejected, thinking who is lost to him? and
  at night, awaking, think who is lost?
Does he too harbor his friendship silent and endless?
  harbor his anguish and passion?

Does some stray reminder, or the casual mention of a
   name, bring the fit back upon him, taciturn and
   deprest?
Does he see himself reflected in me? In these hours,
   does he see the face of his hours reflected?

# FOR YOU O DEMOCRACY

Come, I will make the continent indissoluble,
I will make the most splendid race the sun ever shone
   upon,
I will make divine magnetic lands,
     With the love of comrades,
       With the life-long love of comrades.

I will plant companionship thick as trees along all the
   rivers of America, and along the shores of the great
   lakes, and all over the prairies,
I will make inseparable cities with their arms about
   each other's necks,
     By the love of comrades,
      By the manly love of comrades.

For you these from me, O Democracy, to serve you
   ma femme!
For you, for you I am trilling these songs.

## OF THE TERRIBLE DOUBT OF
## APPEARANCES

Of the terrible doubt of appearances,
Of the uncertainty after all, that we may be deluded,
That may-be reliance and hope are but speculations
    after all,
That may-be identity beyond the grave is a beautiful
    fable only,
May-be the things I perceive, the animals, plants, men,
    hills, shining and flowing waters,
The skies of day and night, colors, densities, forms,
    may-be these are (as doubtless they are) only
    apparitions, and the real something has yet to be
    known,
(How often they dart out of themselves as if to
    confound me and mock me!
How often I think neither I know, nor any man
    knows, aught of them,)
May-be seeming to me what they are (as doubtless
    they indeed but seem) as from my present point of
    view, and might prove (as of course they would)
    nought of what they appear, or nought anyhow,
    from entirely changed points of view;
To me these and the like of these are curiously
    answer'd by my lovers, my dear friends,

When he whom I love travels with me or sits a long
    while holding me by the hand,
When the subtle air, the impalpable, the sense that
    words and reason hold not, surround us and
    pervade us,
Then I am charged with untold and untellable
    wisdom, I am silent, I require nothing further,
I cannot answer the question of appearances or that of
    identity beyond the grave,
But I walk or sit indifferent, I am satisfied,
He ahold of my hand has completely satisfied me.

# WHEN I HEARD AT THE CLOSE OF THE DAY

When I heard at the close of the day how my name
    had been receiv'd with plaudits in the capitol, still it
    was not a happy night for me that follow'd,
And else when I carous'd, or when my plans were
    accomplish'd, still I was not happy,
But the day when I rose at dawn from the bed of
    perfect health, refresh'd, singing, inhaling the ripe
    breath of autumn,
When I saw the full moon in the west grow pale and
    disappear in the morning light,
When I wander'd alone over the beach, and
    undressing bathed, laughing with the cool waters,
    and saw the sun rise,
And when I thought how my dear friend my lover was
    on his way coming, O then I was happy,
O then each breath tasted sweeter, and all that day
    my food nourish'd me more, and the beautiful day
    pass'd well,
And the next came with equal joy, and with the next
    at evening came my friend,
And that night while all was still I heard the waters
    roll slowly continually up the shores,

I heard the hissing rustle of the liquid and sands as
    directed to me whispering to congratulate me,
For the one I love most lay sleeping by me under the
    same cover in the cool night,
In the stillness in the autumn moonbeams his face was
    inclined toward me,
And his arm lay lightly around my breast – and that
    night I was happy.

# I SAW IN LOUISIANA A LIVE-OAK GROWING

I saw in Louisiana a live-oak growing,
All alone stood it and the moss hung down from the
  branches,
Without any companion it grew there uttering joyous
  leaves of dark green,
And its look, rude, unbending, lusty, made me think
  of myself,
But I wonder'd how it could utter joyous leaves
  standing alone there without its friend near, for I
  knew I could not,
And I broke off a twig with a certain number of leaves
  upon it, and twined around it a little moss,
And brought it away, and I have placed it in sight in
  my room,
It is not needed to remind me as of my own dear
  friends,
(For I believe lately I think of little else than of them,)
Yet it remains to me a curious token, it makes me
  think of manly love;
For all that, and though the live-oak glistens there in
  Louisiana solitary in a wide flat space,
Uttering joyous leaves all its life without a friend a
  lover near,
I know very well I could not.

## THIS MOMENT YEARNING AND
## THOUGHTFUL

This moment yearning and thoughtful sitting alone,
It seems to me there are other men in other lands
  yearning and thoughtful,
It seems to me I can look over and behold them in
  Germany, Italy, France, Spain,
Or far, far away, in China, or in Russia or Japan,
  talking other dialects,
And it seems to me if I could know those men I
  should become attached to them as I do to men in
  my own lands,
O I know we should be brethren and lovers,
I know I should be happy with them.

*From* SONG OF THE OPEN ROAD

1.

Afoot and light-hearted I take to the open road,
Healthy, free, the world before me,
The long brown path before me leading wherever I
    choose.

Henceforth I ask not good-fortune, I myself am good-
    fortune,
Henceforth I whimper no more, postpone no more,
    need nothing,

Done with indoor complaints, libraries, querulous
    criticisms,
Strong and content I travel the open road.

The earth, that is sufficient,
I do not want the constellations any nearer,
I know they are very well where they are,
I know they suffice for those who belong to them.

(Still here I carry my old delicious burdens,
I carry them, men and women, I carry them with me
    wherever I go,
I swear it is impossible for me to get rid of them,
I am fill'd with them, and I will fill them in return.)

5.

From this hour I ordain myself loos'd of limits and
    imaginary lines,
Going where I list, my own master total and absolute,
Listening to others, considering well what they say,
Pausing, searching, receiving, contemplating,
Gently, but with undeniable will, divesting myself of
    the holds that would hold me.

I inhale great draughts of space,
The east and the west are mine, and the north and
    the south are mine.

I am larger, better than I thought,
I did not know I held so much goodness.

All seems beautiful to me,
I can repeat over to men and women You have done
    such good to me I would do the same to you,
I will recruit for myself and you as I go,
I will scatter myself among men and women as I go,
I will toss a new gladness and roughness among them,
Whoever denies me it shall not trouble me,
Whoever accepts me he or she shall be blessed and
    shall bless me.

9.

Allons! whoever you are come travel with me!
Traveling with me you find what never tires.

The earth never tires,
The earth is rude, silent, incomprehensible at first,
    Nature is rude and incomprehensible at first,
Be not discouraged, keep on, there are divine things
    well envelop'd,
I swear to you there are divine things more beautiful
    than words can tell.

Allons! we must not stop here,
However sweet these laid-up stores, however
    convenient this dwelling we cannot remain here,
However shelter'd this port and however calm these
    waters we must not anchor here,
However welcome the hospitality that surrounds us we
    are permitted to receive it but a little while.

## 11.

Listen! I will be honest with you,
I do not offer the old smooth prizes, but offer rough
    new prizes,
These are the days that must happen to you:
You shall not heap up what is call'd riches,
You shall scatter with lavish hand all that you earn or
    achieve,
You but arrive at the city to which you were destin'd,
    you hardly settle yourself to satisfaction before you
    are call'd by an irresistible call to depart,
You shall be treated to the ironical smiles and
    mockings of those who remain behind you,
What beckonings of love you receive you shall only
    answer with passionate kisses of parting,
You shall not allow the hold of those who spread their
    reach'd hands toward you.

Allons! the road is before us!
It is safe – I have tried it – my own feet have tried it
    well – be not detain'd!


Let the paper remain on the desk unwritten, and the
    book on the shelf unopen'd!
Let the tools remain in the workshop! let the money
    remain unearn'd!
Let the school stand! mind not the cry of the teacher!
Let the preacher preach in his pulpit! let the lawyer
    plead in the court, and the judge expound the law.

Camerado, I give you my hand!
I give you my love more precious than money,
I give you myself before preaching or law;
Will you give me yourself? will you come travel with
    me?
Shall we stick by each other as long as we live?

*From* CROSSING BROOKLYN FERRY

3.

It avails not, time nor place – distance avails not,
I am with you, you men and women of a generation,
    or ever so many generations hence,
Just as you feel when you look on the river and sky, so
    I felt,
Just as any of you is one of a living crowd, I was one
    of a crowd,
Just as you are refresh'd by the gladness of the river
    and the bright flow, I was refresh'd,
Just as you stand and lean on the rail, yet hurry with
    the swift current, I stood yet was hurried,
Just as you look on the numberless masts of ships and
    the thick-stemm'd pipes of steamboats, I look'd.

I too many and many a time cross'd the river of old,
Watched the Twelfth-month sea-gulls, saw them high
    in the air floating with motionless wings, oscillating
    their bodies,
Saw how the glistening yellow lit up parts of their
    bodies and left the rest in strong shadow,

Saw the slow-wheeling circles and the gradual edging
    toward the south,
Saw the reflection of the summer sky in the water,
Had my eyes dazzled by the shimmering track of
    beams,
Look'd at the fine centrifugal spokes of light round the
    shape of my head in the sunlit water,
Look'd on the haze on the hills southward and south-
    westward,
Look'd on the vapor as it flew in fleeces tinged with
    violet,
Look'd toward the lower bay to notice the vessels
    arriving,
Saw their approach, saw aboard those that were near
    me,
Saw the white sails of schooners and sloops, saw the
    ships at anchor,
The sailors at work in the rigging or out astride the
    spars,
The round masts, the swinging motion of the hulls,
    the slender serpentine pennants,
The large and small steamers in motion, the pilots in
    their pilot-houses,

The white wake left by the passage, the quick
tremulous whirl of the wheels,
The flags of all nations, the falling of them at sunset,
The scallop-edged waves in the twilight, the ladled
cups, the frolicsome crests and glistening,
The stretch afar growing dimmer and dimmer, the
gray walls of the granite storehouses by the docks,
On the river the shadowy group, the big steam-tug
closely flank'd on each side by the barges, the hay-
boat, the belated lighter,
On the neighboring shore the fires from the foundry
chimneys burning high and glaringly into the night,
Casting their flicker of black contrasted with wild red
and yellow light over the tops of houses and down
into the clefts of streets.

# OUT OF THE CRADLE ENDLESSLY ROCKING

Out of the cradle endlessly rocking,
Out of the mocking-bird's throat, the musical shuttle,
Out of the Ninth-month midnight,
Over the sterile sands and the fields beyond, where the
    child leaving his bed wander'd alone, bareheaded,
    barefoot,
Down from the shower'd halo,
Up from the mystic play of shadows twining and
    twisting as if they were alive,
Out from the patches of briers and blackberries,
From the memories of the bird that chanted to me,
From your memories sad brother, from the fitful risings
    and fallings I heard,
From under that yellow half-moon late-risen and
    swollen as if with tears,
From those beginning notes of yearning and love there
    in the mist,
From the thousand responses of my heart never to
    cease,
From the myriad thence-arous'd words,
From the word stronger and more delicious than any,
From such as now they start the scene revisiting,
As a flock, twittering, rising, or overhead passing,

Borne hither, ere all eludes me, hurriedly,
A man, yet by these tears a little boy again,
Throwing myself on the sand, confronting the waves,
I, chanter of pains and joys, uniter of here and
    hereafter,
Taking all hints to use them, but swiftly leaping
    beyond them,
A reminiscence sing.

Once Paumanok,
When the lilac-scent was in the air and Fifth-month
    grass was growing,
Up this seashore in some briers,
Two feather'd guests from Alabama, two together,
And their nest, and four light-green eggs spotted with
    brown,
And every day the he-bird to and fro near at hand,
And every day the she-bird crouch'd on her nest,
    silent, with bright eyes,
And every day I, a curious boy, never too close, never
    disturbing them,
Cautiously peering, absorbing, translating.

*Shine! shine! shine!*
*Pour down your warmth, great sun!*
*While we bask, we two together.*

*Two together!*
*Winds blow south, or winds blow north,*
*Day come white, or night come black,*
*Home, or rivers and mountains from home,*
*Singing all time, minding no time,*
*While we two keep together.*

Till of a sudden,
May-be kill'd, unknown to her mate,
One forenoon the she-bird crouch'd not on the nest,
Nor return'd that afternoon, nor the next,
Nor ever appear'd again.

And thenceforward all summer in the sound of the
  sea,
And at night under the full of the moon in calmer
  weather,
Over the hoarse surging of the sea,
Or flitting from brier to brier by day,
I saw, I heard at intervals the remaining one, the he-
  bird,
The solitary guest from Alabama.

*Blow! blow! blow!*
*Blow up sea-winds along Paumanok's shore;*
*I wait and I wait till you blow my mate to me.*


Yes, when the stars glisten'd,
All night long on the prong of a moss-scallop'd stake,
Down almost amid the slapping waves,
Sat the lone singer wonderful causing tears.
He call'd on his mate,
He pour'd forth the meanings which I of all men
    know.


Yes my brother I know,
The rest might not, but I have treasur'd every note,
For more than once dimly down to the beach gliding,
Silent, avoiding the moonbeams, blending myself with
    the shadows,
Recalling now the obscure shapes, the echoes, the
    sounds and sights after their sorts,
The white arms out in the breakers tirelessly tossing,
I, with bare feet, a child, the wind wafting my hair,
Listen'd long and long.


Listen'd to keep, to sing, now translating the notes,
Following you my brother.

*Soothe! soothe! soothe!*
*Close on its wave soothes the wave behind,*
*And again another behind embracing and lapping, every*
  *one close,*
*But my love soothes not me, not me.*

*Low hangs the moon, it rose late,*
*It is lagging – O I think it is heavy with love, with love.*

*O madly the sea pushes upon the land,*
*With love, with love.*

*O night! do I not see my love fluttering out among the*
  *breakers?*
*What is that little black thing I see there in the white?*

*Loud! loud! loud!*
*Loud I call to you, my love!*
*High and clear I shoot my voice over the waves,*
*Surely you must know who is here, is here,*
*You must know who I am, my love.*

*Low-hanging moon!*
*What is that dusky spot in your brown yellow?*
*O it is the shape, the shape of my mate!*
*O moon do not keep her from me any longer.*

*Land! land! O land!*
*Whichever way I turn, O I think you could give me my*
    *mate back again if you only would,*
*For I am almost sure I see her dimly whichever way I look.*

*O rising stars!*
*Perhaps the one I want so much will rise, will rise with*
    *some of you.*


*O throat! O trembling throat!*
*Sound clearer through the atmosphere!*
*Pierce the woods, the earth,*
*Somewhere listening to catch you must be the one I want.*

*Shake out carols!*
*Solitary here, the night's carols!*
*Carols of lonesome love! death's carols!*
*Carols under that lagging, yellow, waning moon!*
*O under that moon where she droops almost down into the*
    *sea!*
*O reckless despairing carols.*

*But soft! sink low!*
*Soft! let me just murmur,*
*And do you wait a moment you husky-nois'd sea,*
*For somewhere I believe I heard my mate responding to me,*
*So faint, I must be still, be still to listen,*
*But not altogether still, for then she might not come*
   *immediately to me.*

*Hither my love!*
*Here I am! here!*
*With this just-sustain'd note I announce myself to you,*
*This gentle call is for you my love, for you.*

*Do not be decoy'd elsewhere,*
*That is the whistle of the wind, it is not my voice,*
*That is the fluttering, the fluttering of the spray,*
*Those are the shadows of leaves.*

*O darkness! O in vain!*
*O I am very sick and sorrowful.*

*O brown halo in the sky near the moon, drooping upon the*
    *sea!*
*O troubled reflection in the sea!*
*O throat! O throbbing heart!*
*And I singing uselessly, uselessly all the night.*

*O past! O happy life! O songs of joy!*
*In the air, in the woods, over fields,*
*Loved! loved! loved! loved! loved!*
*But my mate no more, no more with me!*
*We two together no more.*

The aria sinking,
All else continuing, the stars shining,
The winds blowing, the notes of the bird continuous
    echoing,
With angry moans the fierce old mother incessantly
    moaning,
On the sands of Paumanok's shore gray and rustling,
The yellow half-moon enlarged, sagging down,
    drooping, the face of the sea almost touching,

The boy ecstatic, with his bare feet the waves, with his
    hair the atmosphere dallying,
The love in the heart long pent, now loose, now at
    last tumultuously bursting,
The aria's meaning, the ears, the soul, swiftly
    depositing,
The strange tears down the cheeks coursing,
The colloquy there, the trio, each uttering,
The undertone, the savage old mother incessantly
    crying,
To the boy's soul's questions sullenly timing, some
    drown'd secret hissing,
To the outsetting bard.
Demon or bird! (said the boy's soul,)
Is it indeed toward your mate you sing? or is it really
    to me?
For I, that was a child, my tongue's use sleeping, now I
    have heard you,
Now in a moment I know what I am for, I awake,
And already a thousand singers, a thousand songs,
    clearer, louder and more sorrowful than yours,
A thousand warbling echoes have started to life within
    me, never to die.

O you singer solitary, singing by yourself, projecting
  me,
O solitary me listening, never more shall I cease
  perpetuating you,
Never more shall I escape, never more the
  reverberations,
Never more the cries of unsatisfied love be absent from
  me,
Never again leave me to be the peaceful child I was
  before what there in the night,
By the sea under the yellow and sagging moon,
The messenger there arous'd, the fire, the sweet hell
  within,
The unknown want, the destiny of me.

O give me the clew! (it lurks in the night here
  somewhere,)
O if I am to have so much, let me have more!

A word then, (for I will conquer it,)
The word final, superior to all,
Subtle, sent up – what is it? – I listen;
Are you whispering it, and have been all the time, you
    sea-waves?
Is that it from your liquid rims and wet sands?

Whereto answering, the sea,
Delaying not, hurrying not,
Whisper'd me through the night, and very plainly
    before daybreak,
Lisp'd to me the low and delicious word death,
And again death, death, death, death,
Hissing melodious, neither like the bird nor like my
    arous'd child's heart,
But edging near as privately for me rustling at my feet,
Creeping thence steadily up to my ears and laving me
    softly all over,
Death, death, death, death, death.

Which I do not forget,
But fuse the song of my dusky demon and brother,
That he sang to me in the moonlight on Paumanok's
    gray beach,
With the thousand responsive songs at random,
My own songs awaked from that hour,
And with them the key, the word up from the waves,
The word of the sweetest song and all songs,
That strong and delicious word which, creeping to my
    feet,
(Or like some old crone rocking the cradle, swathed in
    sweet garments, bending aside,)
The sea whisper'd me.

# AS I EBB'D WITH THE OCEAN OF LIFE

## 1.

As I ebb'd with the ocean of life,
As I wended the shores I know,
As I walk'd where the ripples continually wash you
    Paumanok,
Where they rustle up hoarse and sibilant,
Where the fierce old mother endlessly cries for her
    castaways,
I musing late in the autumn day, gazing off southward,
Held by this electric self out of the pride of which I
    utter poems,
Was seiz'd by the spirit that trails in the lines
    underfoot,
The rim, the sediment that stands for all the water
    and all the land of the globe.

Fascinated, my eyes reverting from the south, dropt, to
    follow those slender windrows,
Chaff, straw, splinters of wood, weeds, and the sea-
    gluten,
Scum, scales from shining rocks, leaves of salt-lettuce,
    left by the tide,
Miles walking, the sound of breaking waves the other
    side of me,
Paumanok there and then as I thought the old
    thought of likenesses,
These you presented to me you fish-shaped island,
As I wended the shores I know,
As I walk'd with that electric self seeking types.

As I wend to the shores I know not,
As I list to the dirge, the voices of men and women
 wreck'd,
As I inhale the impalpable breezes that set in upon
 me,
As the ocean so mysterious rolls toward me closer and
 closer,
I too but signify at the utmost a little wash'd-up drift,
A few sands and dead leaves to gather,
Gather, and merge myself as part of the sands and
 drift.

O baffled, balk'd, bent to the very earth,
Oppress'd with myself that I have dared to open my
 mouth,
Aware now that amid all that blab whose echoes recoil
 upon me I have not once had the least idea who or
 what I am,
But that before all my arrogant poems the real Me
 stands yet untouch'd, untold, altogether unreach'd,
Withdrawn far, mocking me with mock-congratulatory
 signs and bows,
With peals of distant ironical laughter at every word I
 have written,

Pointing in silence to these songs, and then to the
    sand beneath.
I perceive I have not really understood any thing, not
    a single object, and that no man ever can,
Nature here in sight of the sea taking advantage of me
    to dart upon me and sting me,
Because I have dared to open my mouth to sing at all.

3.

You oceans both, I close with you,
We murmur alike reproachfully rolling sands and drift,
    knowing not why,
These little shreds indeed standing for you and me and
    all.

You friable shore with trails of debris,
You fish-shaped island, I take what is underfoot,
What is yours is mine my father.

I too Paumanok,
I too have bubbled up, floated the measureless float,
    and been wash'd on your shores,
I too am but a trail of drift and debris,
I too leave little wrecks upon you, you fish-shaped
    island.

I throw myself upon your breast my father,
I cling to you so that you cannot unloose me,
I hold you so firm till you answer me something.

Kiss me my father,
Touch me with your lips as I touch those I love,
Breathe to me while I hold you close the secret of the
    murmuring I envy.

4.

Ebb, ocean of life, (the flow will return,)
Cease not your moaning you fierce old mother,
Endlessly cry for your castaways, but fear not, deny
    not me,
Rustle not up so hoarse and angry against my feet as I
    touch you or gather from you.

I mean tenderly by you and all,
I gather for myself and for this phantom looking down
    where we lead, and following me and mine.

Me and mine, loose windrows, little corpses,
Froth, snowy white, and bubbles,
(See, from my dead lips the ooze exuding at last,
See, the prismatic colors glistening and rolling,)
Tufts of straw, sands, fragments,
Buoy'd hither from many moods, one contradicting
    another,
From the storm, the long calm, the darkness, the
    swell,
Musing, pondering, a breath, a briny tear, a dab of
    liquid or soil,
Up just as much out of fathomless workings fermented
    and thrown,

A limp blossom or two, torn, just as much over waves
    floating, drifted at random,
Just as much for us that sobbing dirge of Nature,
Just as much whence we come that blare of the cloud-
    trumpets,
We, capricious, brought hither we know not whence,
    spread out before you,
You up there walking or sitting,
Whoever you are, we too lie in drifts at your feet.

# FIRST O SONGS FOR A PRELUDE

First O songs for a prelude,
Lightly strike on the stretch'd tympanum pride and joy
    in my city,
How she led the rest to arms, how she gave the cue,
How at once with lithe limbs unwaiting a moment she
    sprang,
(O superb! O Manhattan, my own, my peerless!
O strongest you in the hour of danger, in crisis! O
    truer than steel!)
How you sprang – how you threw off the costumes of
    peace with indifferent hand,
How your soft opera-music changed, and the drum
    and fife were heard in their stead,
How you led to the war, (that shall serve for our
    prelude, songs of soldiers,)
How Manhattan drum-taps led.

Forty years had I in my city seen soldiers parading,
Forty years as a pageant, till unawares the lady of this
　　teeming and turbulent city,
Sleepless amid her ships, her houses, her incalculable
　　wealth,
With her million children around her, suddenly,
At dead of night, at news from the south,
Incens'd struck with clinch'd hand the pavement.

A shock electric, the night sustain'd it,
Till with ominous hum our hive at daybreak pour'd
　　out its myriads.

From the houses then and the workshops, and
　　through all the doorways,
Leapt they tumultuous, and lo! Manhattan arming.

To the drum-taps prompt,

The young men falling in and arming,

The mechanics arming, (the trowel, the jack-plane, the
blacksmith's hammer, tost aside with precipitation,)

The lawyer leaving his office and arming, the judge
leaving the court,

The driver deserting his wagon in the street, jumping
down, throwing the reins abruptly down on the
horses' backs,

The salesman leaving the store, the boss, book-keeper,
porter, all leaving;

Squads gather everywhere by common consent and
arm,

The new recruits, even boys, the old men show them
how to wear their accoutrements, they buckle the
straps carefully,

Outdoors arming, indoors arming, the flash of the
musket-barrels,

The white tents cluster in camps, the arm'd sentries
around, the sunrise cannon and again at sunset,

Arm'd regiments arrive every day, pass through the
city, and embark from the wharves,

(How good they look as they tramp down to the river,
  sweaty, with their guns on their shoulders!
How I love them! how I could hug them, with their
  brown faces and their clothes and knapsacks cover'd
  with dust!)
The blood of the city up – arm'd! arm'd! the cry
  everywhere,
The flags flung out from the steeples of churches and
  from all the public buildings and stores,
The tearful parting, the mother kisses her son, the son
  kisses his mother,
(Loth is the mother to part, yet not a word does she
  speak to detain him,)
The tumultuous escort, the ranks of policemen
  preceding, clearing the way,
The unpent enthusiasm, the wild cheers of the crowd
  for their favorites,
The artillery, the silent cannons bright as gold, drawn
  along, rumble lightly over the stones,
(Silent cannons, soon to cease your silence,
Soon unlimber'd to begin the red business;)

All the mutter of preparation, all the determin'd
    arming,
The hospital service, the lint, bandages and medicines,
The women volunteering for nurses, the work begun
    for in earnest, no mere parade now;
War! an arm'd race is advancing! the welcome for
    battle, no turning away;
War! be it weeks, months, or years, an arm'd race is
    advancing to welcome it.

Mannahatta a-march – and it's O to sing it well!
It's O for a manly life in the camp.

And the sturdy artillery,
The guns bright as gold, the work for giants, to serve
    well the guns,
Unlimber them! (no more as the past forty years for
    salutes for courtesies merely,
Put in something now besides powder and wadding.)

And you lady of ships, you Mannahatta,
Old matron of this proud, friendly, turbulent city,
Often in peace and wealth you were pensive or
    covertly frown'd amid all your children,
But now you smile with joy exulting old Mannahatta.

## EIGHTEEN SIXTY-ONE

Arm'd year – year of the struggle,
No dainty rhymes or sentimental love verses for you
    terrible year,
Not you as some pale poetling seated at a desk lisping
    cadenzas piano,
But as a strong man erect, clothed in blue clothes,
    advancing, carrying a rifle on your shoulder,
With well-gristled body and sunburnt face and hands,
    with a knife in the belt at your side,
As I heard you shouting loud, your sonorous voice
    ringing across the continent,
Your masculine voice O year, as rising amid the great
    cities,
Amid the men of Manhattan I saw you as one of the
    workmen, the dwellers in Manhattan,
Or with large steps crossing the prairies out of Illinois
    and Indiana,
Rapidly crossing the West with springy gait, and
    descending the Alleghanies,          ,
Or down from the great lakes or in Pennsylvania, or
    on deck along the Ohio river,

Or southward along the Tennessee or Cumberland
    rivers, or at Chattanooga on the mountain top,
Saw I your gait and saw I your sinewy limbs clothed in
    blue, bearing weapons, robust year,
Heard your determin'd voice launch'd forth again and
    again,
Year that suddenly sang by the mouths of the round-
    lipp'd cannon,
I repeat you, hurrying, crashing, sad, distracted year.

# VIGIL STRANGE I KEPT ON THE FIELD ONE NIGHT

Vigil strange I kept on the field one night;

When you my son and my comrade dropt at my side
that day,

One look I but gave which your dear eyes return'd
with a look I shall never forget,

One touch of your hand to mine O boy, reach'd up as
you lay on the ground,

Then onward I sped in the battle, the even-contested
battle,

Till late in the night reliev'd to the place at last again I
made my way,

Found you in death so cold, dear comrade, found your
body son of responding kisses, (never again on earth
responding,)

Bared your face in the starlight, curious the scene, cool
blew the moderate night-wind,

Long there and then in vigil I stood, dimly around me
the battlefield spreading,

Vigil wondrous and vigil sweet there in the fragrant
silent night,

But not a tear fell, not even a long-drawn sigh, long,
long I gazed,

Then on the earth partially reclining sat by your side
    leaning my chin in my hands,
Passing sweet hours, immortal and mystic hours with
    you dearest comrade – not a tear, not a word,
Vigil of silence, love and death, vigil for you my son
    and my soldier,
As onward silently stars aloft, eastward new ones
    upward stole,
Vigil final for you brave boy, (I could not save you,
    swift was your death,
I faithfully loved you and cared for you living, I think
    we shall surely meet again,)
Till at latest lingering of the night, indeed just as the
    dawn appear'd,
My comrade I wrapt in his blanket, envelop'd well his
    form,
Folded the blanket well, tucking it carefully over head
    and carefully under feet,
And there and then and bathed by the rising sun, my
    son in his grave, in his rude-dug grave I deposited,
Ending my vigil strange with that, vigil of night and
    battle-field dim,
Vigil for boy of responding kisses, (never again on
    earth responding,)

Vigil for comrade swiftly slain, vigil I never forget, how
    as day brighten'd,
I rose from the chill ground and folded my soldier well
    in his blanket,
And buried him where he fell.

# THE WOUND-DRESSER

## 1.

An old man bending I come among new faces,
Years looking backward resuming in answer to
  children,
Come tell us old man, as from young men and
  maidens that love me,
(Arous'd and angry, I'd thought to beat the alarum,
  and urge relentless war,
But soon my fingers fail'd me, my face droop'd and I
  resign'd myself,
To sit by the wounded and soothe them, or silently
  watch the dead;)
Years hence of these scenes, of these furious passions,
  these chances,
Of unsurpass'd heroes, (was one side so brave? the
  other was equally brave;)
Now be witness again, paint the mightiest armies of
  earth,
Of those armies so rapid so wondrous that saw you to
  tell us?
What stays with you latest and deepest? of curious
  panics,
Of hard-fought engagements or sieges tremendous
  what deepest remains?

2.

O maidens and young men I love and that love me,
What you ask of my days those the strangest and
    sudden your talking recalls,
Soldier alert I arrive after a long march cover'd with
    sweat and dust,
In the nick of time I come, plunge in the fight, loudly
    shout in the rush of successful charge,
Enter the captur'd works – yet lo, like a swift-running
    river they fade,
Pass and are gone they fade – I dwell not on soldiers'
    perils or soldiers' joys,
(Both I remember well – many the hardships, few the
    joys, yet I was content.)

But in silence, in dreams' projections,
While the world of gain and appearance and mirth
    goes on,
So soon what is over forgotten, and waves wash the
    imprints off the sand,
With hinged knees returning I enter the doors, (while
    for you up there,
Whoever you are, follow without noise and be of
    strong heart.)

Bearing the bandages, water and sponge,
Straight and swift to my wounded I go,
Where they lie on the ground after the battle brought
in,
Where their priceless blood reddens the grass the
ground,
Or to the rows of the hospital tent, or under the
roof'd hospital,
To the long rows of cots up and down each side I
return,
To each and all one after another I draw near, not
one do I miss,
An attendant follows holding a tray, he carries a
refuse pail,
Soon to be fill'd with clotted rags and blood, emptied,
and fill'd again.

I onward go, I stop,
With hinged knees and steady hand to dress wounds,
I am firm with each, the pangs are sharp yet
unavoidable,
One turns to me his appealing eyes – poor boy! I never
knew you,
Yet I think I could not refuse this moment to die for
you, if that would save you.

## 3.

On, on I go, (open doors of time! open hospital doors!)
The crush'd head I dress, (poor crazed hand tear not
   the bandage away,)
The neck of the cavalry-man with the bullet through
   and through I examine,
Hard the breathing rattles, quite glazed already the
   eye, yet life struggles hard,
(Come sweet death! be persuaded O beautiful death!
In mercy come quickly.)

From the stump of the arm, the amputated hand,
I undo the clotted lint, remove the slough, wash off
   the matter and blood,
Back on his pillow the soldier bends with curv'd neck
   and side-falling head,
His eyes are closed, his face is pale, he dares not look
   on the bloody stump,
And has not yet look'd on it.

I dress a wound in the side, deep, deep,
But a day or two more, for see the frame all wasted
   and sinking,
And the yellow-blue countenance see.

I dress the perforated shoulder, the foot with the
    bullet-wound,
Cleanse the one with a gnawing and putrid gangrene,
    so sickening, so offensive,
While the attendant stands behind aside me holding
    the tray and pail.

I am faithful, I do not give out,
The fractur'd thigh, the knee, the wound in the
    abdomen,
These and more I dress with impassive hand, (yet deep
    in my breast a fire, a burning flame.)

Thus in silence in dreams' projections,
Returning, resuming, I thread my way through the
   hospitals,
The hurt and wounded I pacify with soothing hand,
I sit by the restless all the dark night, some are so
   young,
Some suffer so much, I recall the experience sweet and
   sad,
(Many a soldier's loving arms about this neck have
   cross'd and rested,
Many a soldier's kiss dwells on these bearded lips.)

# RECONCILIATION

Word over all, beautiful as the sky,
Beautiful that war and all its deeds of carnage must in
time be utterly lost,
That the hands of the sisters Death and Night
incessantly softly wash again, and ever again, this
soil'd world;
For my enemy is dead, a man divine as myself is dead,
I look where he lies white-faced and still in the coffin –
I draw near,
Bend down and touch lightly with my lips the white
face in the coffin.

# AS I LAY WITH MY HEAD IN YOUR LAP
## CAMERADO

As I lay with my head in your lap camerado,
The confession I made I resume, what I said to you
    and the open air I resume,
I know I am restless and make others so,
I know my words are weapons full of danger, full of
    death,
For I confront peace, security, and all the settled laws,
    to unsettle them,
I am more resolute because all have denied me than I
    could ever have been had all accepted me,
I heed not and have never heeded either experience,
    cautions, majorities, nor ridicule,
And the threat of what is call'd hell is little or nothing
    to me,
And the lure of what is call'd heaven is little or
    nothing to me;
Dear camerado! I confess I have urged you onward
    with me, and still urge you, without the least idea
    what is our destination,
Or whether we shall be victorious, or utterly quell'd
    and defeated.

## TO A CERTAIN CIVILIAN

Did you ask dulcet rhymes from me?
Did you seek the civilian's peaceful and languishing
   rhymes?
Did you find what I sang erewhile so hard to follow?
Why I was not singing erewhile for you to follow, to
   understand – nor am I now;
(I have been born of the same as the war was born,
The drum-corps' rattle is ever to me sweet music, I
   love well the martial dirge,
With slow wail and convulsive throb leading the
   officer's funeral;)
What to such as you anyhow such a poet as I?
   therefore leave my works,
And go lull yourself with what you can understand,
   and with piano-tunes,
For I lull nobody, and you will never understand me.

# WHEN LILACS LAST IN THE DOORYARD BLOOM'D

## 1.

When lilacs last in the dooryard bloom'd,
And the great star early droop'd in the western sky in
   the night,
I mourn'd, and yet shall mourn with ever-returning
   spring.

Ever-returning spring, trinity sure to me you bring,
Lilac blooming perennial and drooping star in the
   west,
And thought of him I love.

## 2.

O powerful western fallen star!
O shades of night – O moody, tearful night!
O great star disappear'd – O the black murk that hides
  the star!
O cruel hands that hold me powerless – O helpless
  soul of me!
O harsh surrounding cloud that will not free my soul.

3.

In the dooryard fronting an old farm-house near the
    white-wash'd palings,
Stands the lilac-bush tall-growing with heart-shaped
    leaves of rich green,
With many a pointed blossom rising delicate, with the
    perfume strong I love,
With every leaf a miracle – and from this bush in the
    dooryard,
With delicate-color'd blossoms and heart-shaped leaves
    of rich green,
A sprig with its flower I break.

## 4.

In the swamp in secluded recesses,
A shy and hidden bird is warbling a song.
Solitary the thrush,
The hermit withdrawn to himself, avoiding the
    settlements,
Sings by himself a song.

Song of the bleeding throat,
Death's outlet song of life, (for well dear brother I
    know,
If thou wast not granted to sing thou would'st surely
    die.)

## 5.

Over the breast of the spring, the land, amid cities,
Amid lanes and through old woods, where lately the
    violets peep'd from the ground, spotting the gray
    debris,
Amid the grass in the fields each side of the lanes,
    passing the endless grass,
Passing the yellow-spear'd wheat, every grain from its
    shroud in the dark-brown fields uprisen,
Passing the apple-tree blows of white and pink in the
    orchards,
Carrying a corpse to where it shall rest in the grave,
Night and day journeys a coffin.

Coffin that passes through lanes and streets,
Through day and night with the great cloud darkening
    the land,
With the pomp of the inloop'd flags with the cities
    draped in black,
With the show of the States themselves as of crape-
    veil'd women standing,
With processions long and winding and the flambeaus
    of the night,
With the countless torches lit, with the silent sea of
    faces and the unbared heads,
With the waiting depot, the arriving coffin, and the
    sombre faces,
With dirges through the night, with the thousand
    voices rising strong and solemn,
With all the mournful voices of the dirges pour'd
    around the coffin,
The dim-lit churches and the shuddering organs –
    where amid these you journey,
With the tolling tolling bells' perpetual clang,
Here, coffin that slowly passes,
I give you my sprig of lilac.

## 7.

(Nor for you, for one alone,
Blossoms and branches green to coffins all I bring,
For fresh as the morning, thus would I chant a song
   for you
    O sane and sacred death.

All over bouquets of roses,
O death, I cover you over with roses and early lilies,
But mostly and now the lilac that blooms the first,
Copious I break, I break the sprigs from the bushes,
With loaded arms I come, pouring for you,
For you and the coffins all of you O death.)

8.

O western orb sailing the heaven,
Now I know what you must have meant as a month
    since I walk'd,
As I walk'd in silence the transparent shadowy night,
As I saw you had something to tell as you bent to me
    night after night,
As you droop'd from the sky low down as if to my
    side, (while the other stars all look'd on,)
As we wander'd together the solemn night, (for
    something I know not what kept me from sleep,)
As the night advanced, and I saw on the rim of the
    west how full you were of woe,
As I stood on the rising ground in the breeze in the
    cool transparent night,
As I watch'd where you pass'd and was lost in the
    netherward black of the night,
As my soul in its trouble dissatisfied sank, as where
    you sad orb,
Concluded, dropt in the night, and was gone.

9.

Sing on there in the swamp,
O singer bashful and tender, I hear your notes, I hear
  your call,
I hear, I come presently, I understand you,
But a moment I linger, for the lustrous star has
  detain'd me,
The star my departing comrade holds and detains me.

10.

O how shall I warble myself for the dead one there I
    loved?
And how shall I deck my song for the large sweet soul
    that has gone?
And what shall my perfume be for the grave of him I
    love?

Sea-winds blown from east and west,
Blown from the Eastern sea and blown from the
    Western sea, till there on the prairies meeting,
These and with these and the breath of my chant,
I'll perfume the grave of him I love.

## 11.

O what shall I hang on the chamber walls?
And what shall the pictures be that I hang on the
    walls,
To adorn the burial-house of him I love?

Pictures of growing spring and farms and homes,
With the Fourth-month eve at sundown, and the gray
    smoke lucid and bright,
With floods of the yellow gold of the gorgeous,
    indolent, sinking sun, burning, expanding the air,
With the fresh sweet herbage under foot, and the pale
    green leaves of the trees prolific,
In the distance the flowing glaze, the breast of the
    river, with a wind-dapple here and there,
With ranging hills on the banks, with many a line
    against the sky, and shadows,
And the city at hand with dwellings so dense, and
    stacks of chimneys,
And all the scenes of life and the workshops, and the
    workmen homeward returning.

## 12.

Lo, body and soul – this land,
My own Manhattan with spires, and the sparkling and
   hurrying tides, and the ships,
The varied and ample land, the South and the North
   in the light, Ohio's shores and flashing Missouri,
And ever the far-spreading prairies cover'd with grass
   and corn.

Lo, the most excellent sun so calm and haughty,
The violet and purple morn with just-felt breezes,
The gentle soft-born measureless light,
The miracle spreading bathing all, the fulfill'd noon,
The coming eve delicious, the welcome night and the
   stars,
Over my cities shining all, enveloping man and land.

## 13.

Sing on, sing on you gray-brown bird,
Sing from the swamps, the recesses, pour your chant
  from the bushes,
Limitless out of the dusk, out of the cedars and pines.

Sing on dearest brother, warble your reedy song,
Loud human song, with voice of uttermost woe.

O liquid and free and tender!
O wild and loose to my soul – O wondrous singer!
You only I hear – yet the star holds me, (but will soon
  depart,)
Yet the lilac with mastering odor holds me.

Now while I sat in the day and look'd forth,
In the close of the day with its light and the fields of
    spring, and the farmers preparing their crops,
In the large unconscious scenery of my land with its
    lakes and forests,
In the heavenly aerial beauty, (after the perturb'd
    winds and the storms,)
Under the arching heavens of the afternoon swift
    passing, and the voices of children and women,
The many-moving sea-tides, and I saw the ships how
    they sail'd,
And the summer approaching with richness, and the
    fields all busy with labor,
And the infinite separate houses, how they all went
    on, each with its meals and minutia of daily usages,
And the streets how their throbbings throbb'd, and
    the cities pent – lo, then and there,
Falling upon them all and among them all, enveloping
    me with the rest,
Appear'd the cloud, appear'd the long black trail,
And I knew death, its thought, and the sacred
    knowledge of death.

Then with the knowledge of death as walking one side
    of me,
And the thought of death close-walking the other side
    of me,
And I in the middle as with companions, and as
    holding the hands of companions,
I fled forth to the hiding receiving night that talks not,
Down to the shores of the water, the path by the
    swamp in the dimness,
To the solemn shadowy cedars and ghostly pines so
    still.

And the singer so shy to the rest receiv'd me,
The gray-brown bird I know receiv'd us comrades
    three,
And he sang the carol of death, and a verse for him I
    love.

From deep secluded recesses,
From the fragrant cedars and the ghostly pines so still,
·Came the carol of the bird.

And the charm of the carol rapt me,
As I held as if by their hands my comrades in the
    night,
And the voice of my spirit tallied the song of the bird.

Come lovely and soothing death,
Undulate round the world, serenely arriving, arriving,
In the day, in the night, to all, to each,
Sooner or later delicate death.

Prais'd be the fathomless universe,
For life and joy, and for objects and knowledge curious,
And for love, sweet love – but praise! praise! praise!
For the sure-enwinding arms of cool-enfolding death.

Dark mother always gliding near with soft feet,
Have none chanted for thee a chant of fullest welcome?
Then I chant it for thee, I glorify thee above all,
I bring thee a song that when thou must indeed come, come
  unfalteringly.

Approach strong deliveress,
When it is so, when thou hast taken them I joyously sing
  the dead,
Lost in the loving floating ocean of thee,
Laved in the flood of thy bliss O death.

From me to thee glad serenades,
Dances for thee I propose saluting thee, adornments and
  feastings for thee,
And the sights of the open landscape and the high-spread
  sky are fitting,
And life and the fields, and the huge and thoughtful night.

The night in silence under many a star,
The ocean shore and the husky whispering wave whose
  voice I know,
And the soul turning to thee O vast and well-veil'd death,
And the body gratefully nestling close to thee.

Over the tree-tops I float thee a song,
Over the rising and sinking waves, over the myriad fields
  and the prairies wide,
Over the dense-pack'd cities all and the teeming wharves
  and ways,
I float this carol with joy, with joy to thee O death.

15.

To the tally of my soul,
Loud and strong kept up the gray-brown bird,
With pure deliberate notes spreading filling the night.

Loud in the pines and cedars dim,
Clear in the freshness moist and the swamp-perfume,
And I with my comrades there in the night.

While my sight that was bound in my eyes unclosed,
As to long panoramas of visions.

And I saw askant the armies,
I saw as in noiseless dreams hundreds of battle-flags,
Borne through the smoke of the battles and pierc'd
    with missiles I saw them,
And carried hither and yon through the smoke, and
    torn and bloody,
And at last but a few shreds left on the staffs, (and all
    in silence,)
And the staffs all splinter'd and broken.

I saw battle-corpses, myriads of them,
And the white skeletons of young men, I saw them,
I saw the debris and debris of all the slain soldiers of
the war,
But I saw they were not as was thought,
They themselves were fully at rest, they suffer'd not,
The living remain'd and suffer'd, the mother suffer'd,
And the wife and the child and the musing comrade
suffer'd,
And the armies that remain'd suffer'd.

## 16

Passing the visions, passing the night,
Passing, unloosing the hold of my comrades' hands,
Passing the song of the hermit bird and the tallying
    song of my soul,
Victorious song, death's outlet song, yet varying ever-
    altering song,
As low and wailing, yet clear the notes, rising and
    falling, flooding the night,
Sadly sinking and fainting, as warning and warning,
    and yet again bursting with joy,
Covering the earth and filling the spread of the
    heaven,
As that powerful psalm in the night I heard from
    recesses,
Passing, I leave thee lilac with heart-shaped leaves,
I leave thee there in the dooryard, blooming, returning
    with spring.

I cease from my song for thee,
From my gaze on thee in the west, fronting the west,
    communing with thee,
O comrade lustrous with silver face in the night.

Yet each to keep and all, retrievements out of the
  night,
The song, the wondrous chant of the gray-brown bird,
And the tallying chant, the echo arous'd in my soul,
With the lustrous and drooping star with the
  countenance full of woe,
With the holders holding my hand nearing the call of
  the bird,
Comrades mine and I in the midst, and their memory
  ever to keep, for the dead I loved so well,
For the sweetest, wisest soul of all my days and lands –
  and this for his dear sake,
Lilac and star and bird twined with the chant of my
  soul,
There in the fragrant pines and the cedars dusk and
  dim.

# O CAPTAIN! MY CAPTAIN!

O Captain! my Captain! our fearful trip is done,
The ship has weather'd every rack, the prize we sought
  is won,
The port is near, the bells I hear, the people all
  exulting,
While follow eyes the steady keel, the vessel grim and
  daring:
  But O heart! heart! heart!
    O the bleeding drops of red,
   Where on the deck my Captain lies,
      Fallen cold and dead.

O Captain! my Captain! rise up and hear the bells;
Rise up – for you the flag is flung – for you the bugle
  trills,
For you bouquets and ribbon'd wreaths – for you the
  shores a-crowding,
For you they call, the swaying mass, their eager faces
  turning;
  Here Captain! dear father!
    This arm beneath your head!
     It is some dream that on the deck,
        You've fallen cold and dead.

My Captain does not answer, his lips are pale and still,

My father does not feel my arm, he has no pulse nor
    will,

The ship is anchor'd safe and sound, its voyage closed
    and done,

From fearful trip the victor ship comes in with object
    won;

    Exult O shores, and ring O bells!

      But I with mournful tread,

        Walk the deck my Captain lies,

          Fallen cold and dead.

# THIS COMPOST

## 1.

Something startles me where I thought I was safest,
I withdraw from the still woods I loved,
I will not go now on the pastures to walk,
I will not strip the clothes from my body to meet my
  lover the sea,
I will not touch my flesh to the earth as to other flesh
  to renew me.

O how can it be that the ground itself does not
  sicken?
How can you be alive you growths of spring?
How can you furnish health you blood of herbs, roots,
  orchards, grain?
Are they not continually putting distemper'd corpses
  within you?
Is not every continent work'd over and over with sour
  dead?

Where have you disposed of their carcasses?
Those drunkards and gluttons of so many generations?
Where have you drawn off all the foul liquid and
  meat?
I do not see any of it upon you to-day, or perhaps I
  am deceiv'd,
I will run a furrow with my plough, I will press my
  spade through the sod and turn it up underneath,
I am sure I shall expose some of the foul meat.

2.

Behold this compost! behold it well!
Perhaps every mite has once form'd part of a sick
    person – yet behold!
The grass of spring covers the prairies,
The bean bursts noiselessly through the mould in the
    garden,
The delicate spear of the onion pierces upward,
The apple-buds cluster together on the apple-branches,
The resurrection of the wheat appears with pale visage
    out of its graves,
The tinge awakes over the willow-tree and the
    mulberry-tree,
The he-birds carol mornings and evenings while the
    she-birds sit on their nests,
The young of poultry break through the hatch'd eggs,
The new-born of animals appear, the calf is dropt from
    the cow, the colt from the mare,
Out of its little hill faithfully rise the potato's dark
    green leaves,
Out of its hill rises the yellow maize-stalk, the lilacs
    bloom in the dooryards,
The summer growth is innocent and disdainful above
    all those strata of sour dead.

What chemistry!

That the winds are really not infectious,

That this is no cheat, this transparent green-wash of
the sea which is so amorous after me,

That it is safe to allow it to lick my naked body all
over with its tongues,

That it will not endanger me with the fevers that have
deposited themselves in it,

That all is clean forever and forever,

That the cool drink from the well tastes so good,

That blackberries are so flavorous and juicy,

That the fruits of the apple-orchard and the orange-
orchard, that melons, grapes, peaches, plums, will
none of them poison me,

That when I recline on the grass I do not catch any
disease,

Though probably every spear of grass rises out of what
was once a catching disease.

Now I am terrified at the Earth, it is that calm and
  patient,
It grows such sweet things out of such corruptions,
It turns harmless and stainless on its axis, with such
  endless successions of diseas'd corpses,
It distills such exquisite winds out of such infused
  fetor,
It renews with such unwitting looks its prodigal,
  annual, sumptuous crops,
It gives such divine materials to men, and accepts such
  leavings from them at last.

## 8.

The sleepers are very beautiful as they lie unclothed,
They flow hand in hand over the whole earth from
    east to west as they lie unclothed,
The Asiatic and African are hand in hand, the
    European and American are hand in hand,
Learn'd and unlearn'd are hand in hand, and male
    and female are hand in hand,
The bare arm of the girl crosses the bare breast of her
    lover, they press close without lust, his lips press her
    neck,
The father holds his grown or ungrown son in his
    arms with measureless love, and the son holds the
    father in his arms with measureless love,
The white hair of the mother shines on the white
    wrist of the daughter,
The breath of the boy goes with the breath of the
    man, friend is inarm'd by friend,
The scholar kisses the teacher and the teacher kisses
    the scholar, the wrong'd is made right,
The call of the slave is one with the master's call, and
    the master salutes the slave,

The felon steps forth from the prison, the insane
  becomes sane, the suffering of sick persons is
  reliev'd,
The sweatings and fevers stop, the throat that was
  unsound is sound, the lungs of the consumptive are
  resumed, the poor distress'd head is free,
The joints of the rheumatic move as smoothly as ever,
  and smoother than ever,
Stiflings and passages open, the paralyzed become
  supple,
The swell'd and convuls'd and congested awake to
  themselves in condition,
They pass the invigoration of the night and the
  chemistry of the night, and awake.

I too pass from the night,
I stay a while away O night, but I return to you again
    and love you.
Why should I be afraid to trust myself to you?
I am afraid, I have been well brought forward by you,
I love the rich running day, but I do not desert her in
    whom I lay so long,
I know not how I came of you and I know not where I
    go with you, but I know I came well and shall go
    well.

I will stop only a time with the night, and rise betimes,
I will duly pass the day O my mother, and duly return
    to you.

## OF HIM I LOVE DAY AND NIGHT

Of him I love day and night I dream'd I heard he was
  dead,
And I dream'd I went where they had buried him I
  love, but he was not in that place,
And I dream'd I wander'd searching among burial-
  places to find him,
And I found that every place was a burial-place;
The houses full of life were equally full of death, (this
  house is now,)
The streets, the shipping, the places of amusement, the
  Chicago, Boston, Philadelphia, the Mannahatta,
  were as full of the dead as of the living,
And fuller, O vastly fuller of the dead than of the living;
And what I dream'd I will henceforth tell to every
  person and age,
And I stand henceforth bound to what I dream'd,
And now I am willing to disregard burial-places and
  dispense with them,
And if the memorials of the dead were put up
  indifferently everywhere, even in the room where I
  eat or sleep, I should be satisfied,
And if the corpse of any one I love, or if my own
  corpse, be duly render'd to powder and pour'd in
  the sea, I shall be satisfied,
Or if it be distributed to the winds I shall be satisfied.

# EXCELSIOR

Who has gone farthest? for I would go farther,

And who has been just? for I would be the most just
person of the earth,

And who most cautious? for I would be more cautious,

And who has been happiest? O I think it is I – I think
no one was ever happier than I,

And who has lavish'd all? for I lavish constantly the
best I have,

And who proudest? for I think I have reason to be the
proudest son alive – for I am the son of the brawny
and tall-topt city,

And who has been bold and true? for I would be the
boldest and truest being of the universe,

And who benevolent? for I would show more
benevolence than all the rest,

And who has receiv'd the love of the most friends? for
I know what it is to receive the passionate love of
many friends,

And who possesses a perfect and enamour'd body? for
I do not believe any one possesses a more perfect or
enamour'd body than mine,

And who thinks the amplest thoughts? for I would
surround those thoughts,

And who has made hymns fit for the earth? for I am
mad with devouring ecstasy to make joyous hymns
for the whole earth.

## AS THE TIME DRAWS NIGH

As the time draws nigh glooming a cloud,
A dread beyond of I know not what darkens me.

I shall go forth,
I shall traverse the States awhile, but I cannot tell
  whither or how long,
Perhaps soon some day or night while I am singing my
  voice will suddenly cease.

O book, O chants! must all then amount to but this?
Must we barely arrive at this beginning of us? – and
  yet it is enough, O soul;
O soul, we have positively appear'd – that is enough.

# AS AT THY PORTALS ALSO DEATH

As at thy portals also death,
Entering thy sovereign, dim, illimitable grounds,
To memories of my mother, to the divine blending,
    maternity,
To her, buried and gone, yet buried not, gone not
    from me,
(I see again the calm benignant face fresh and beautiful
    still,
I sit by the form in the coffin,
I kiss and kiss convulsively again the sweet old lips,
    the cheeks, the closed eyes in the coffin;)
To her, the ideal woman, practical, spiritual, of all of
    earth, life, love, to me the best,
I grave a monumental line, before I go, amid these
    songs,
And set a tombstone here.

# MY LEGACY

The business man the acquirer vast,
After assiduous years surveying results, preparing for
 departure,
Devises houses and lands to his children, bequeaths
 stocks, goods, funds for a school or hospital,
Leaves money to certain companions to buy tokens,
 souvenirs of gems and gold.

But I, my life surveying, closing,
With nothing to show to devise from its idle years,
Nor houses nor lands, nor tokens of gems or gold for
 my friends,
Yet certain remembrances of the war for you, and after
 you,
And little souvenirs of camps and soldiers, with my
 love,
I bind together and bequeath in this bundle of songs.

## SO LONG!

To conclude, I announce what comes after me.

I remember I said before my leaves sprang at all,
I would raise my voice jocund and strong with
   reference to consummations.

When America does what was promis'd,
When through these States walk a hundred millions of
   superb persons,
When the rest part away for superb persons and
   contribute to them,
When breeds of the most perfect mothers denote
   America,
Then to me and mine our due fruition.

I have press'd through in my own right,
I have sung the body and the soul, war and peace
   have I sung, and the songs of life and death,
And the songs of birth, and shown that there are
   many births.

I have offer'd my style to every one, I have journey'd
    with confident step;
While my pleasure is yet at the full I whisper *So long!*
And take the young woman's hand and the young
    man's hand for the last time.

I announce natural persons to arise,
I announce justice triumphant,
I announce uncompromising liberty and equality,
I announce the justification of candor and the
    justification of pride.

I announce that the identity of these States is a single
    identity only,
I announce the Union more and more compact,
    indissoluble,
I announce splendors and majesties to make all the
    previous politics of the earth insignificant.

I announce adhesiveness, I say it shall be limitless,
    unloosen'd,
I say you shall yet find the friend you were looking for.

I announce a man or woman coming, perhaps you are
    the one, (*So long!*)
I announce the great individual, fluid as Nature,
    chaste, affectionate, compassionate, fully arm'd.

I announce a life that shall be copious, vehement,
    spiritual, bold,
I announce an end that shall lightly and joyfully meet
    its translation.

I announce myriads of youths, beautiful, gigantic,
    sweet-blooded,
I announce a race of splendid and savage old men.

O thicker and faster – (*So long!*)
O crowding too close upon me,
I foresee too much, it means more than I thought,
It appears to me I am dying.

Hasten throat and sound your last,
Salute me – salute the days once more. Peal the old
    cry once more.

Screaming electric, the atmosphere using,
At random glancing, each as I notice absorbing,
Swiftly on, but a little while alighting,
Curious envelop'd messages delivering,
Sparkles hot, seed ethereal down in the dirt drooping,
Myself unknowing, my commission obeying, to
    question it never daring,
To ages and ages yet the growth of the seed leaving,
To troops out of the war arising, they the tasks I have
    set promulging,
To women certain whispers of myself bequeathing,
    their affection me more clearly explaining,
To young men my problems offering - no dallier I -
    I the muscle of their brains trying,
So I pass, a little time vocal, visible, contrary,
Afterward a melodious echo, passionately bent for,
    (death making me really undying,)
The best of me then when no longer visible, for
    toward that I have been incessantly preparing.

What is there more, that I lag and pause and crouch
    extended with unshut mouth?
Is there a single final farewell?

My songs cease, I abandon them,
From behind the screen where I hid I advance
    personally solely to you.

Camerado, this is no book,
Who touches this touches a man,
(Is it night? are we here together alone?)
It is I you hold and who holds you,
I spring from the pages into your arms – decease calls
    me forth.

O how your fingers drowse me,
Your breath falls around me like dew, your pulse lulls
    the tympans of my ears,
I feel immerged from head to foot,
Delicious, enough.
Enough O deed impromptu and secret,
Enough O gliding present – enough O summ'd-up
    past.

Dear friend whoever you are take this kiss,
I give it especially to you, do not forget me,
I feel like one who has done work for the day to retire
  awhile,
I receive now again of my many translations, from my
  avataras ascending, while others doubtless await me,
An unknown sphere more real than I dream'd, more
  direct, darts awakening rays about me, *So long!*
Remember my words, I may again return,
I love you, I depart from materials,
I am as one disembodied, triumphant, dead.

## GOOD-BYE MY FANCY!

Good-bye my Fancy!
Farewell dear mate, dear love!
I'm going away, I know not where,
Or to what fortune, or whether I may ever see you
   again,
So Good-bye my Fancy.

Now for my last – let me look back a moment;
The slower fainter ticking of the clock is in me,
Exit, nightfall, and soon the heart-thud stopping.

Long have we lived, joy'd, caress'd together;
Delightful! – now separation – Good-bye my Fancy.

Yet let me not be too hasty,
Long indeed have we lived, slept, filter'd, become
  really blended into one;
Then if we die we die together, (yes, we'll remain one,)
If we go anywhere we'll go together to meet what
  happens,
May-be we'll be better off and blither, and learn
  something,
May-be it is yourself now really ushering me to the
  true songs, (who knows?)
May-be it is you the mortal knob really undoing,
  turning – so now finally,
Good-bye – and hail! my Fancy.